Strange ...

ATLANTIS

KYLA STEINKRAUS

BLACK RABBIT BOOKS

Bolt is published by Black Rabbit Books
P.O. Box 3263, Mankato, Minnesota, 56002.
www.blackrabbitbooks.com
Copyright © 2018 Black Rabbit Books

Marysa Storm, editor; Grant Gould, interior
designer; Michael Sellner, cover designer;
Omay Ayres, photo researcher

Library of Congress Cataloging-in-Publication Data
Names: Steinkraus, Kyla, author.
Title: Atlantis / by Kyla Steinkraus.
Description: Mankato, Minnesota : Black Rabbit Books, [2018] | Series: Bolt.
Strange . . . But True? | Includes bibliographical references and index. |
Audience: Ages: 9-12. | Audience: Grades: 4 to 6.
Identifiers: LCCN 2016049988 (print) | LCCN 2016054332 (ebook) | ISBN
9781680721812 (library binding) | ISBN 9781680722451 (e-book) | ISBN
9781680724783 (paperback)
Subjects: LCSH: Atlantis (Legendary place)–Juvenile literature.
Classification: LCC GN751 .S83 2018 (print) | LCC GN751 (ebook) | DDC
001.94-dc23
LC record available at https://lccn.loc.gov/2016049988

Printed in the United States at CG Book Printers,
North Mankato, Minnesota, 56003. 3/17

Contents

CHAPTER 1

The Legend of

In 2009, Richard Freund searched for the lost island of Atlantis. He looked for it in Spain. He and his crew looked above and below ground for **remains**. While searching, they found two **figurines**. Could they be from Atlantis? Had they found the lost island?

For many years, people like Freund have looked for Atlantis.

People first heard the story of Atlantis around 360 BC. It came from Plato. He was a Greek thinker. He said Atlantis was an **ancient** island. It existed more than 10,000 years ago. He said the sea god Poseidon made it.

Pride and Punishment

Stories say the people of Atlantis had **advanced** technology. They were powerful too. They built beautiful buildings. But they were not good people. They were full of **pride**. They started many wars.

Plato said their actions angered the gods. They punished the people. They sent earthquakes and floods to Atlantis. It sank beneath the sea. It took only a day and night to disappear.

Poseidon's son Atlas was king of Atlantis.

CENTER ISLAND

BRIDGES

HARBORS

10

RINGS OF LAND AND SEA CIRCLING A PALACE

PALACE

TEMPLES

LAND GOOD FOR GROWING PLANTS

CHAPTER 2

History of

For thousands of years, few people knew Plato's story. In 1881, Ignatius Donnelly wrote a book about Atlantis. People grew interested in the island. They wanted to know more!

ATLANTIS IN POP CULTURE
(SINCE 1900)

books
TV shows
video games
comics
movies   10+

10

55+

35+

30+

25+

20   30   40   50   60   13

Sea

Baltic

ENGLAND
London

GERMANY

PRUSS

St George's Chan.

Paris

Vienn

English Chan.

FRANCE

AUSTR

C.Charles

Newfoundland

B. of
Biscay

E

St Lawrence

C.Breton I.

Madrid

Rome

G.of Venice

N.Scotia

Lisbon

Cod

A T L A N T I C

Madeira Is.

ITALY

Azores or
Western Is.

Str.of Gibralter

Algiers

Sicily

M E D I T E R R A N E

k B.

Canary Is.

Tripoli

Ba

A N

C.Blanco

Tropic F of

Ca

A

F

R.Senegal

pe Verde Is.

Timbuctoo

L.Tchad

C.Verde

R

N. SEA

Sierra
Leone

S O U D A N

uraccas

G U I N E A

MBIA

GU

C.Palmas

Biafra

IV

mazon

G.of Guinea
XII

T H

Equ

R.Congo

Congo

St.Phillip

C

About
60%
of Americans believe
advanced civilizations
like Atlantis
once existed.

Where Is It?

Plato said Atlantis was past the Pillars of Hercules. These huge stones are near the Mediterranean Sea. Many people think Atlantis was near there. Others aren't so sure. They believe Atlantis was somewhere else.

Believing in Mysteries

About
36%
of Americans believe UFOs are spaceships.

About
21%
of Americans believe Bigfoot is real.

SEARCHING FOR ATLANTIS

There are many places people believe Atlantis could be found.

GREENLAND

SPAIN

CANARY ISLANDS

CARIBBEAN

BOLIVIA

SCANDINAVIA

GERMANY

TURKEY

SANTORINI

ANTARCTICA

17

CHAPTER 3

Could Atlantis Be Real?

Believers say Plato wrote many details of Atlantis. Why would he give so many details about a fake place?

Some think Atlantis is in the Mediterranean Sea. There is an island called Santorini there. More than 3,500 years ago, a volcano there **erupted**. The eruption was huge. It caused **tsunamis**. Most of the island was destroyed. • • • • • • • • • •

In 1967, people found remains of a city on Santorini. The people who lived there were smart. They had been powerful too. They practiced bull leaping. Stories say people on Atlantis did too. Some people think Santorini was Atlantis.

Others think the lost city could be somewhere else. Some, like Freund, think it could be in Spain.

CHAPTER 4

Is a Mystery

Other people believe Plato's Atlantis was **symbolic**. He was really talking about his own people. He lived in Athens, Greece. He thought the city's people were full of pride. He wanted them to change.

Some say Santorini couldn't be the lost city. Atlantis existed long before Santorini.

Not ATLANTIS?

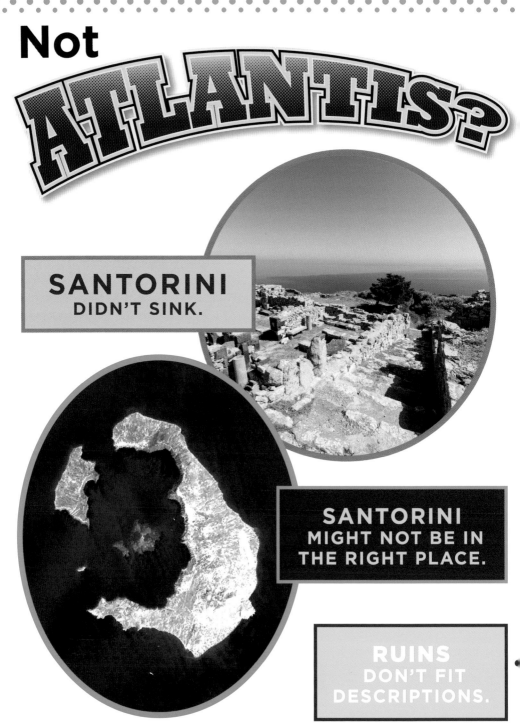

SANTORINI
DIDN'T SINK.

SANTORINI
MIGHT NOT BE IN
THE RIGHT PLACE.

RUINS
DON'T FIT
DESCRIPTIONS.

Nonbelievers also say Santorini isn't Atlantis because it didn't sink. It didn't disappear. It was only damaged.

People say there are no other stories about Atlantis in history. Plato is the only one who told the story. They also believe explorers wouldn't miss such large ruins.

Fact or Fiction?

Many think Atlantis is only a story. They wonder why it hasn't been found yet. They ask why no ruins fit the descriptions.

Believers don't think every fact has to match. Some believe Santorini is the lost island. Others think Atlantis is still waiting to be found.

Will we ever know for sure?

Some think the people of Atlantis were aliens.
This theory explains the city's advanced technology.

Believe It or Not?

Answer the questions below. Then add up your points to see if you believe.

1 Are there mysteries in the ocean?

A. There sure are! (3 points)

B. I don't know. (2 points)

C. We've already explored the whole world. (1 point)

2 There are reports that sunken ruins have been found. What do you think?

A. It must be Atlantis! (3 points)

B. Sounds interesting. (2 points)

C. That's not Atlantis! (1 point)

3 Look at the diagram on pages 10–11. What do you think?

A. I want to live there! (3 points)

B. I'm not sure it's real. (2 points)

C. A city that cool must be fake!

(1 point)

· · · · · · · · · · · · ·

3 points

There's no way Atlantis is real.

4–8 points

Maybe it's real. But then again, maybe it's not.

9 points

You're a total believer!

advanced (ad-VANSD)—being beyond others in progress

ancient (AYN-shunt)—from a time long ago

erupt (ih-RUPT)—to suddenly explode

figurine (fig-yuh-REEN)—a small statue

pride (PRAHYD)—a high opinion of one's own worth

remains (ri-MEYNZ)—what is left after everything else has gone or disappeared

ruins (ROO-ins)—remains of a building that has been destroyed

symbolic (sim-BOL-ik)—something that stands for something else

temple (TEM-puhl)—a building for religious practice

tsunami (tsoo-NAH-mee)—an unusually large sea wave produced by an earthquake or volcanic eruption

BOOKS

Karst, Ken. *Atlantis*. Enduring Mysteries. Mankato, MN: Creative Education, 2015.

Lassieur, Allison. *Is Atlantis Real?* Unexplained: What's the Evidence? Mankato, MN: Amicus, 2016.

Michels, Troy. *Atlantis*. The Unexplained. Minneapolis: Bellwether Media, 2011.

WEBSITES

The Lost City of Atlantis
www.easyscienceforkids.com/all-about-the-lost-city-of-atlantis/

The Lost City of Atlantis
www.kidzworld.com/article/960-history-the-lost-city-of-atlantis

Where Is the Lost City of Atlantis?
www.wonderopolis.org/wonder/where-is-the-lost-city-of-atlantis/

INDEX